WITHDRAWN

A Spiritual Diary for Saints

& Not-So-Saintly

Ruthe White

Harvest House Publishers
Irvine, California 92714

Acknowledgement

To Claude, my husband, for loving me through both
the . . .
   SAINTLY AND NOT SO SAINTLY moments of
   my life.

Contents

Strength For Sinners And ... Saints

Do I Have to Feel
Spiritual Today?

Do I have to feel spiritual today, Lord?

Is it alright if I tell you I am tired, too mentally tired to care?

Now, don't misunderstand me! I am not asking for a "leave of absence" from right and wrong.

I just want to be human!

To let my head catch up with my heart. One seems always to be getting ahead of the other.

Either my head wants to rule my heart, or my heart my head. Why is that?

"You were not that way when I created you," God said, "so who flubbed up?"

"Lean on, trust and be confident in the Lord with all your heart and mind, and do not rely on your own insight or understanding" (Proverbs 3:5, AMP).

Jog, Jog, Jog

Jog, jog, jog!

That's all I hear. The doctor tells me to jog for my health. I think he is dead wrong. In my opinion, he is trying to kill me, to get rid of another of his "mini-pause" patients.

I don't have time to run!

This morning I rolled from between the sheets with full intention of making my first mile. Sleepily I put one foot through the leg of what I thought was my sweat-suit. The legs came out short, and the waistline sagged to my knees. I fumbled with the buttons wondering when I had sewn the extra one on. But then I do those things sometimes.

Having managed to button the thing, I soon dis-covered I had fastened myself into my husband's pa-jama top.

Up and down, over the bed and under its covers, I searched, trying to find the lost tennis shoe that kept evading me. Finally, there was nothing left to do but borrow. So after pulling three pairs of woolen socks onto my feet, I tied myself securely into a pair of man-size "teeny-runners."

Then . . . I remembered, I should drink my orange juice. It's good for the system I am told.

I stumbled over the vacuum cleaner on my way into the garage, hoping to find one can of instant energy hidden in the deep-freeze. Sure enough, there it was, waiting to be opened.

Just as the freezer door slammed, something soft brushed across the toe of my shoe. I jumped straight up into the air and started running. Right out into the yard I went, yelling "help" at the top of my voice. Suddenly, I knew the neighbors were watching.

When I had finished explaining I was running for my health, one of the men looked at me, nodded his head, and said:

"Lady, please keep running!"

"Let us strip off anything that slows us down or holds us back, and especially those sins that wrap themselves so tightly around our feet and trip us up; and let us run with patience the . . . race that God has set before us" (Hebrews 12:1).

Share My Cup

Thanks, God, for sharing my cup of sorrow.

I drank from it until I could drink no more.

Why did you ask to "sip" from my broken vessel? I would liked to have poured its substance into a fine china teacup before offering it to you.

But, you just kept whispering, "Let us drink together," as you lifted my cup to your mouth.

What a delightful surprise to find there was none left. You drank of my sorrow to the very last drop.

Why, Lord, had I not given it to you before?

"Look! I have been standing at the door and I am constantly knocking. If anyone hears me calling him and opens the door, I will come in and fellowship with him and he with me" (Revelation 3:20).

Mud Pots and Mud Pies

Why do I always expect angel food from earthen vessels, or spiritual souffle from mud pots?

Did God not tell us we are clay? Just plain mud in the potter's hand! If so, we should look only for mud pies coming from such common receptacles.

Not so!

The best wine was poured from clay pots at the marriage of Cana in Galilee. The container is not the problem!

The secret lies in its ability to be filled, right to the brim; then, to be poured out that others might drink from its contents.

Listen, I hear the Lord speaking. He is urging me to pour, to give of that which He has given me, to pour it out quickly, before its aroma is lost . . .

. . . Tainted by the smell of the MUD POT where it stayed too long!

"Six stone waterpots were standing there; they were used for Jewish ceremonial purposes and held perhaps twenty to thirty gallons each. Then Jesus told the servants to fill them to the brim with water. When this was done he said, 'Dip some out and take it to the master of ceremonies' " (John 2:6).

All Steamed Up!

Looking through my kitchen window, it appears as if a thick fog is blanketing the sky. Moisture is hugging close to the windowpane, dripping, obscuring my vision.

Strange how the fog affects me!

It brings with it the feeling of being "boxed in" by some mysterious element of nature. There is the urge to protect oneself, to break loose from its limitations.

Yesterday was different! The air was vibrantly alive. The spring breeze reached out with a thousand arms caressing the earth, holding me silently spellbound.

Why should my mood change so quickly from the openness of yesterday's sunshine to the closeness of today's fog?

Could all of this be an indicator pointing to the fickleness of my nature? Is my personality little more than an emotional barometer masuring degrees of outside circumstances; or simply reacting to the humidity of life's changes?

I hope not!

"Wait . . . I see a burst of sunlight through the window. That wasn't fog at all."

P.S.

So sorry, God, for blaming nature. But how was I to know the teakettle had steamed up my kitchen window?

"And don't murmur against God and his dealings with you" (I Corinthians 10:10).

Cat and Mouse

A motley, brown-beiged cat shared her lunch break with me today. She scooted under my board gate and hopped right up onto the patio beside me.

A squirming field mouse was clamped in her mouth between the upper bicuspid and the lower something or other. It's tail was dangling back and forth in a slapping motion, teasing at the long whiskers on the cat's mouth.

Suddenly my peanut butter lost its flavor. The soda cracker turned all leathery to my taste. Every reflex I had went into motion! Both feet flew into the air, then under my "posterior." I just sat there afraid to move.

The stray cat tossed her prey up and down into the air. She was making a game of her victim. When the tiny mouse would try to run away, the long paws of her captor would pull her back into its grasp. Twice the little one almost succeeded in its attempt to get away.

Not so!

With one big lunge the house was swept into the mouth of its predator. Soon there were no signs of life remaining.

Then, I clenched my teeth and shuddered.

When I had returned to reasoning, I slowly unfolded my tense muscles, from their lotus-like positon, and headed for the water hose.

Why had I not thought of that before? Now it was too late to do little more than think.

Was it self-preservation that had numbed my senses? Or was it an attitude of total indifference?

Even so, I could do nothing but pray:

"Please, God, keep me from the sin of apathy. Let me give more to others than just a few pieces of my own protected ego.

"But if any one has this world's goods—resources for sustaining life—and sees his brother and fellow believer in need, yet closes his heart of compassion against him, how can the love of God live and remain in him?" (I John 3:17, AMP).

My Creepin' Charlie

My Creepin' Charlie quit creepin'. Its scraggly leaves curled up, lost their color and dropped to the floor. I pampered it, watered the thing a little too much and sang to it.

Maybe the singing was the final blow; the fact that I have a "tin ear" for music is well known among my friends. But does a plant know?

After having done all those things, it seemed the once living organism was destined to go back to the soil from whence it came.

Finally, there was only one thing left to try: I began pouring vitamins into the depleted soil, hoping to coax its leafy tendrils back to life. Within a few days the limp, milky branches were lifting their heads. They took on a firm, icy-green appearance. New leaves began pushing through from what looked like a once lifeless plant.

Would you believe, the near-dead Creepin' Charlie responded so quickly to the proper chemicals it was soon ready to be admired, enjoyed again!

P.S.
Lord, teach me to deal with the self-deficiencies of my inner life, to feed the inner fibers of my soul, rather than to serve the external nicety of expediency.

"He who covers his transgression will not prosper, but whoever confesses and forsakes his sins shall obtain mercy" (Proverb 28:13).

Doorkeeper

The inner part of me is crying out to God! Inside this human frame there is a longing, a deep longing, to offer, whatever there is of me, to His cause.

But it is hard!

I am afraid, fearful of my own weaknesses; maybe even thinking what I have to give God is not quite-good-enough for His acceptance.

I wonder? Do I imagine that He accepts nothing less than perfection; could I be waiting until I think I have reached that impossible state before offering myself to Him?

Oh! how I long for someone, just anyone to help me. For out of these inadequacies I have turned to human flesh for support. And I have found none! People are busy, doing their own things, building their self-ego, even as I try to do. Yet, they pass me by, as I them, without a thought of where the other may be hurting. Perhaps, I appear strong to them. The Lord knows I am really not; inside I am weak, very weak!

Sometimes I feel the mental geniuses and the physically strong always walk ahead of me. They seem to pass through the open doors of opportunity, unaware of my long struggle in working, waiting for my turn; I need a chance to break loose from this cocoon of inferiority.

Yet, to blame others for what I am, or am not, is such an easy way out. So, I refuse to transfer that responsibility over to another, not even to God who made me like I am.

Yesterday's disappointment will not stop me! What I was then is no excuse for what I am today. Instead of sitting down I WILL get up, and with every bit of energy I can muster I WILL as a not-so saintly saint reach for my impossible dream.

With one deep breath I get up, struggling to stand on my own two feet. But I am standing! Steps are coming

...Wait...I see a DOOR...it is open...wide open
...not closed, as I had thought. Someone is standing
there. It is the Lord and I hear him saying:

"I know you well; you aren't strong, but you
have tried to obey and have not denied my Name.
Therefore I have opened a door to you that no man
can shut" (Revelations 3:8).

P.S. "Forgive me, Lord, I forgot you are the DOOR-
KEEPER and the DOOR!

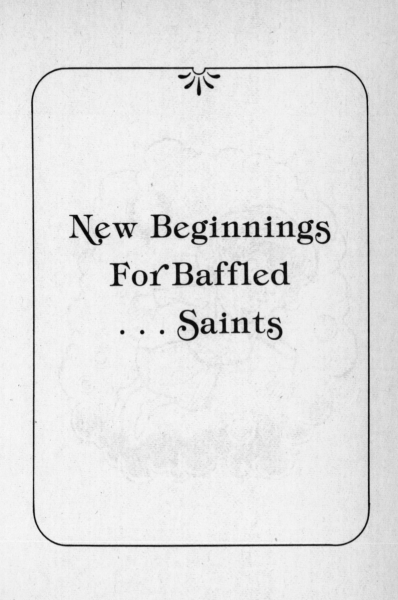

New Beginnings
For Baffled
... Saints

Ugh It's A Tough Day

God, do you know where I am, or do you even care? There are a thousand questions on my mind as I view the earth through this airplane window, looking out across your great big universe.

I wonder about life; what it is all about? Could the God who made all of this be interested in me?

I feel so small compared to the world around me. It is as if I am lost in space, cut loose from the laws of gravitation, temporarily suspended in time to await my turn for landing.

Soon my feet will touch the earth's surface to once again begin running, pushing with all the other people against time. Surely life is more than all of this!

Maybe, it is my lack of spirituality that makes this such a tough day; that causes me to question you as I do.

But, I seem to remember that King David struggled with some of the same problems. For he said:

"When I look up into the night skies and see the work of your fingers—the moon and the stars you have made—I cannot understand how you can bother with mere puny man, to pay attention to him! And yet you have made him a little lower than the angels, and placed a crown of glory upon his head" (Psalm 8:3, TLB).

P.S. Thanks, David, for being human too!

More of Whom?

"Oh! that I had a thousand arms to reach the needy, to touch those in hospitals and to serve humanity," I prayed.

I kept visualizing myself like an octopus with arms reaching out, going into places I could not go with present human limitations.

Suddenly the air grew silent!

God whispered to my heart and said:

"Stop that muttering!

The world has too much of you already. What they really need is more of what I can do through you. And that means more of me and less of you."

. . . and I said,

"Yes, Lord!"

"He must become greater and greater, and I must become less and less" (John 3:30).

Teach Me Honesty

"Please, God, teach me honesty!"

I confess that my not-so-good nature keeps the spiriual balloon of my life deflated much of the time. When I feel like boasting or reach some great mountain peak of perfection. I soon discover my ego.

I find I'm just lost in the fog, with my head in the air, afraid to admit my need of help.

I don't want to pretend I have all the problems of life solved, when truthfully they have had my head in a spin.

So, I ask you to keep me from the temptation of "air bubble" Christianity. Teach me to be true to the people around me. While others may not choose to agree with me, may they never be able to say,

"She was dishonest in her relationship with me."

"Be decent and true in everything you do so that all can approve your behavior " (Romans 13:13).

Potpourri of Junk

Two blown out televisions are staring up at me like ghosts in the night. Hidden behind them is a badly worn vacuum cleaner and an antique piano stool. (It's unvarnished head once lay buried beneath the debris of an old church attic.)

Each day I remind myself of their possible usefulness. I promise to pull out the bad tubes from the television set, replace them with new ones, and varnish and sand the old piano stool.

But another day comes and goes while the work remains undone. In the meantime, here I sit at a make-believe desk in my garage/office among this menagerie of collectable paint cans and mop buckets.

Now, I am wondering: Why would I want to hoard all of this potpourri of nothingness? Can it be these are prodders to my inner self?

P.S.

Dear God, do you see me as being antiquated? Do I have coverings of hate and prejudice that defy your workmanship?

I hope not!

"Please keep my inner soul from hoarding the trivia of life; and . . . from wearing out and blowing up at the same time."

"That out of his glorious, unlimited resources he will give you the mighty inner strengthening of his Holy Spirit " (Ephesians 3:16).

Recycled

Living in my "fantasy house" had been so much fun. That is, until someone came along and knocked my egotistical props right out from under me.

I was enjoying the imaginary thrill of exploring its rooms, the excitement of its pleasures and the fleeting moments of make-believe that are not really meaningful at all.

Suddenly someone came along and "bumped" into my weak structure; leaving me devastated, standing alone amidst the debris, clutching the "broken doll" of my self-ego.

Now I am ashamed and wonder what to do. I feel like a child whose favorite toy is torn to bits.

Perhaps I should stoop and pick up the pieces. Salvage them. Maybe even put them back together again.

No, I dare not!

I must relinquish them to the "Master of Time."

Dump them in the rubbish heap of past experience.

Surely there is something here that is worth saving!

"What! Is that you, God?"

"You say, you want to RECYCLE this mess into something useful, and meaningful . . . unrecognizable?"

"To all who mourn in Israel he will give:

> *Beauty for ashes;*
> *Joy instead of mourning;*
> *Praise instead of heaviness "*
> *(Isaiah 61:3).*

What About
The Highs And Lows?

The low tide of the ocean pulled its watery curtain away from the sandy windows of the seashore. In the shallow water of its beaches a sea gull stood knee-deep bathing, savoring each fleeting moment of rest. A rest from the rolling tide!

Children laughed together building bridges in the sand, knowing full well their dream castles would soon be washed away. They were not troubled by the approaching "HIGH TIDE." Life for them was too exciting at the moment.

So it is, we cannot always be struggling against the rising crest of life's "HIGH TIDES." There are times we need to sit, build dream castles, wade into the calm serenity of today's blessing and bask in the feeling of its ecstasy.

For life is strange, somewhat like the ocean tide. We know even when the tide is low the ocean is yet full. It has just pulled its watery curtain of tears from the shoreline of our hearts, to give us a time of freedom from the tug of the next "BIG WAVE."

"He gathers the waters of the sea as in a bottle; He puts the deeps in storage places" (Psalm 33:7, AMP).

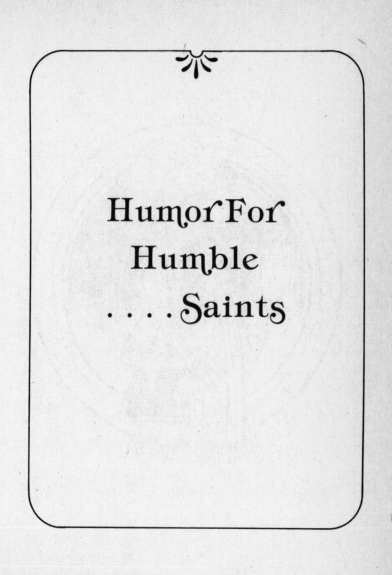

Humor For Humble .... Saints

Looney Birds

Is it true birds of a feather flock together?

Well, one found me the other day. There I was standing in line with a group of other women at a large ecumenical church meeting. One of the female vultures started right for me. You can always tell when they are about to land. They look like they are hunting for prey, as they stalk back-and-forth eyeing over the prospects.

She walked right up to me and asked, "Honey, are you a minister?" Then she interrupted before giving me time to answer, "No."

Her face got all twisted up as if in deep contemplated thought. After some few moments of quiet silence, a bright thought lit up her "psuedo-pious" face.

"Well", she said, "In the last days, God has promised to pour his spirit out on ALL flesh." Then she turned and walked away.

I still do not understand the element of her surprise whether it was good or bad. I think she might have had her doubts about my flesh and God's spirit being able to rest upon it.

One thing for which I am most grateful. . .
"THE LORD I SERVE LOOKS ON THE HEART!"

"But the Lord said . . . 'Don't judge by a man's face or height, . . . I don't make decisions the way you do!' Men judge by the outward appearance, but I look at a man's thoughts and intentions" (I Samuel 16:7).

It Was a Soapy Day

I tried my luck at making lye soap the other day. Having been given a big package of pork fat and being a farm girl, I figured that would be the way to use it.

When I first started the project, I had mental images of snow-white bars, beautifully wrapped in cellophane to be given as gifts to all my city friends.

Well, it didn't happen as I had expected. Instead of bars, I had nothing more than globules of fat.

What could have gone wrong?

The directions said: "Stir slowly to keep from separating." I figured if they said, "stir," beating it with a mixer would be better.

The stirring stage was to have lasted 10 to 20 minutes, after which time it should reach the consistency of honey. One hour of mixing produced nothing more than something akin to syrup.

So, I decided to try another can of lye. That didn't sound right either since it threw the other proportions off. I went back to the lard can throwing in another batch of fat to even-out the mixture.

Suddenly, the odor of grease and lye was about to choke me!

I had hoped my husband would not return home in time to catch me in the middle of the mess. But, he did! He stalked right through the kitchen just as I was about to pour some of his musk oil into the mixture.

"This will make it smell better," I said to myself.

"Dear, can't you find anything better to do on a Saturday other than to make soap?" he patiently inquired.

My conscience was hurting over using his favorite perfume. I felt like a child needing a spanking! So, since I had used his stuff, it seemed only fair I use some of my "fu-fu" oil. I grabbed the bottle and poured a few dabs of concentrated aroma into the pot. By this time, the kitchen had begun to smell like burnt grease in a perfume factor.

I still couldn't hold any promise for the soap to gel; the next best thing seemed to be to bottle it and call the formula a new kind of shampoo. Instead, I just poured it in a pan, took it to the garage and forgot about the whole thing.

A few days later when I got around to checking on the concoction, I discovered a pan full of hard, snow-white bars awaiting me. Boy, the "99% pure" people have nothing on me now.

P.S.

Lord, what am I going to tell the lady who asked for the recipe?

"... though you wash yourself with lye and use much soap, yet your iniquity and guilt are still ... before Me" (Jeremiah 2:22, AMP).

Ugly Duckling

"Give me the natural color nail polish," I said, slapping a well worn hand onto the cosmetic counter. It had no sooner hit the display before being grabbed by an eager salesperson.

"Look Alice, what can we do with this woman's hands?" one lady inquired of the other.

"Huh," she muttered, looking straight at me, "You have a real problem!"

"Oh dear, wonder if I am loosing my nails from digging in the flower beds without gloves?" I asked myself.

"Your skin is dry, very dry," the bifocaled woman said. She stood there rubbing the crooked nail on my index finger, while the other lady, a chic blonde, ran her velvety smooth hand over my calloused one.

"I got this finger caught in the car door . . ."

Before I could explain, one of them began massaging the second and third fingers on my right hand.

"See this one, it got caught in the sewing machine. That's why it looks square."

"Honey, your skin is just drinking up this cream moisture," the younger one of the two said, ignoring my previous statement.

"Alice, do you think our mink oil will perk up the wrinkles around her eyes?"

"Your color is sallow too, maybe this will help." Grabbing a jar of powder in one hand, eye shadow, mascara and rouge in the other, she started in on me.

"This lipstick you are wearing is much too light. If you will let us give you this bright red color, it will draw attention away from your sagging jaw lines," they went on to say.

Then, one of them took a brush in her hand, pressed it against my chin and started painting. "Just going to accentuate that lower lip. It's much too thin."

By this time people were standing looking, waiting for the miracle to emerge. I had begun to feel faint. Having already been convinced of being little more than an "ugly duckling," I knew I could never make it in a world of beautiful women.

"May I have my nail polish?" I pleaded.

"Oh, did you want nail polish?"

She reached for a round bottle of nail enamel and piled it on top of a stack of other cosmetics, as she began computerizing my bill.

I could see it was going to take every bit of my grocery money . . . and then some. So, I started digging through safety pins, gum wrappers and old letters in search of my wallet. After scraping up every penny lost in the lining of my purse, I laid the money for the bill on the counter and walked away.

That night at the dinner table, my daughter looked at me and said: "I thought you went grocery shopping today; why do we have to eat these leftovers?"

"Someday you will understand. Right now, just eat . . . and tonight you'll do the dishes . . . I just had a manicure."

"Don't be concerned about [your] outward [appearance]—or beautiful clothes, or hair arrangement. Be beautiful inside, in your hearts, with the lasting charm of a gentle and quiet spirit which is so precious to God" (I Peter 3:3).

Car Wash

"Lady, back that car out of here!" the attendant yelled at me. Then he flung my car door wide open causing water to drench me from all directions.

"Why, when I am halfway through the car wash will the man not permit me to go on?" I inquired of myself. But when one is sitting under a fountain of water, it is no time to argue the point. And I didn't! I shifted my Red Mustang II into reverse gear as the man had demanded. The car began slowly inching its way backward.

(Have you ever tried backing out of a car wash? Well, it ain't easy!)

The incident occurred when I decided to experience the "new fangled" car wash that had just been installed in our not-too-industrialized city. The one stop service was designed for "filling up and washing up" at the same location. This seemed to be a shortcut from my weekly do-it-yourself project, which involved an enormous amount of effort; to say nothing of the mop buckets, dish rags and household detergent used.

My car had been pushing "E" for days. It sputtered, coughing up the last drop of gasoline, and coasted into the driveway. The car came to a stop right beside two shiny red pumps. The blazing sun reflected against the fine dust that had settled on my car's windshield.

Soon a bulgy, middle-aged woman attendant came bouncing from behind the building. She was wearing shorter-than-short-shorts. Her haltered blouse looked as if it were hanging in midair. A floppy oversized straw hat shaded her weather-beaten face.

"Can I help ya?" she asked.

"Fill 'er up," I answered.

She struggled to get the gas cap off. Then the lady pushed the long necked nozzle into the tank of my car. I watched her as she squeezed the hose handle, trying to get every ounce of petrol into it she could.

"I'll have a car wash, too," I told her.

She stuck a red flag on my radio antenna and motioned for me to get in line behind two other drivers with equally dirty automobiles. There was an overhead sign that read:

"Take your hand off the wheel, foot off the brake and roll up all windows."

Those directions were plain enough for me to understand; but they did not say whether or not I was to turn off the car's motor. So, I just followed close behind the car ahead of me, moving up as the attendant signaled to us.

Very soon I discovered both myself and the car were being dragged by a chain into a tin-frame building. A thousand soapy fingers were pulling us into their grasp. Strips of wet cloth started beating against the windshield. A rolling brush was ready to "gobble" us up.

I panicked!

My foot hit the brake as I grabbed the steering wheel hoping to save my life.

"Lady, take your hands off the wheel," the man yelled at me.

"Should I turn off the motor?"

"I said, take your hand off that wheel, get your foot off the brake," he screamed back at me in not-too-nice language.

Suddenly the left door of my car flew open! There stood the angry attendant, his hair drenched. Liquid bubbles were running off his long nose. Water was pouring in upon me from all directions as the long felt strips slapped back-and-forth at me.

It was as if I were trapped in the mouth of the great Niagara, except for the rolling brushes.

After shifting the vehicle in reverse gear, it started coasting backwards. Just as the front bumper cleared the entrance hookups, the man pushed a button to stop the pulley.

"You get out of there and stand right here," the man said as he pointed to the sidewalk.

I stopped dead in my tracks and I stood there watching as my little red car was being eaten up with soap suds and clanging equipment.

The lady in the haltered blouse was watching the incident as she pumped gasoline into the car of another customer.

"Do you see that woman over there? She is crazy!" The duchess of asphalt told the young couple who had just driven up. (I discovered later they attend my weekly practical Christian living class. Wow! how appropriate.)

Then the battered woman yelled at me:

"Look, you had better go catch your car!"

There it was, headed for a busy intersection. I took out running just as fast as my feet would carry me . . . (that is with high heel shoes on) . . . wet hair and all.

I waited two whole weeks before trying the process again. When I did that same weathered looking lady slithered her way from behind the shaded building to meet me. I waited to see if she would signal the owner that I was back.

She didn't.

"Will there be anything else?" she asked after filling my gas tank to the overflow point.

"Yes, I'll have a car wash, please!"

Just as my front wheels clicked onto the track, I reached down, shut off the motor, put both feet in the air, my hands on my head and rode the car through to the finish line.

The old gal in the shorter-than-short-shorts just stood there shaking her head. I wonder what she whispered in the ear of the attendant when I got out of sight!

P.S. Lord, do you suppose it also bothers some of my husband's parishioners?

"Oh, wash me, cleanse me from this guilt. Let me be pure again. For I admit my shameful deed—it haunts me day and night" (Psalm 51:2).

Sale-ing Season

I realized at this year's annual ministers' meeting that it is a time when the Reverends wear their gaudiest neckties. (Those they dare not wear in their own pulpits.)

For the parsons' wives, it is a fashion show of their latest "sale"-ing bargains. Each woman scrounges for months getting her best duds together, as she tries to match her last year's skirt with this year's blouse. She might even sneak a new purse in from her already meager grocery budget.

In my case it was different! I had started designing a dress three summers before the big event. In the meantime that material was ripped out, basted together and sewn more times than I have fingers. What of it? I fugure at $1.50 for three yards, 50 cents a year ain't being extravagant!

Well, that half-finished original was dragged out of the closet and finished for the big event. It was packed along with all of my other Sunday best and taken to the coast for the meeting. I had planned to strut a bit that year knowing no one else would have a dress like mine.

Wouldn't you know, the weather was too cold for me to wear my summer original.

After coming home, a visiting relative started rummaging through my closet and found the dress.

"Aunt Ruthe, where did you get this designer's . . . (calling the name of a well-known clothes designer) . . . garment," she inquired.

Now I am in a jam! Where does a preacher's wife wear it? If my husband's parishioners think I am paying too much for my clothes, they will want to cut his salary. "He is earning too much," they will say.

"Oh well, there will be another preacher's convention

next year . . . but it will be out of style . . . Come to think of it, I can wear it most anywhere then. If it's out of style, no one will care.

"And why worry about your clothes? Look at the field lilies! They don't worry about theirs" (Matthew 6:28).

"And if God cares so wonderfully for flowers that are here today and gone tomorrow, won't he surely care for you? O men of little faith?" (Mathew 6:30).

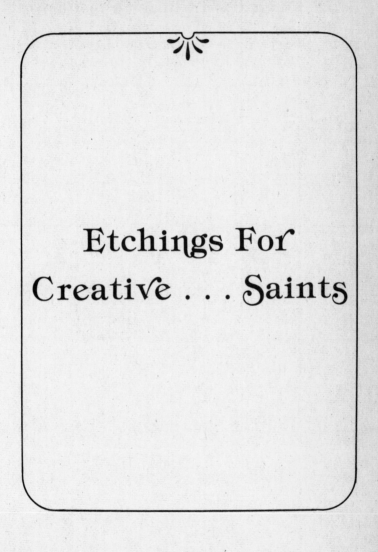

Etchings For
Creative . . . Saints

Angel Unaware

An angel came to my door today!
She had no wings, nor white flowing garments.
  Her beauty was not in what she was wearing.
For she was poor, almost shoddy, but clean.
  Yet, there was a beauty about her.
An inner glow working outwardly,
  Turning everything she touched into a thing of
    beauty.
Her presence came unannounced, unexpectedly,
  She left my house quietly, without clamor for
    attention.

I know the woman was an angel,
Because she gave so much of herself to me.
  There was a feeling of confidence and trust,
Both, in God and others, as she shared with me.
  She spoke ill of no one, criticized no one,
Her only purpose for coming was to bless, . . . and give,
  And she did exactly that.

  *"Don't forget to be kind to strangers, for some
who have done this have entertained angels without realizing it"* (Hebrews 13:2).

I Knocked and Found the Key

I ASKED . . .

That I might receive:
He gave grace sufficient to bear my load;
Strength that sustained me in weakness, and the ability to trust in His Wisdom.

I sought as He said SEEK . . .

I found:
That through my effort of searching I discovered spiritual secrets. Secrets that were once hidden from me as a casual asker. My involvement in the search opened new avenues of self-awareness. A finding of myself as a part of God's Divine Plan.

I KNOCKED . . .

Something opened:
Something inside of me was unlocked; it was as if the KEY had been found in the SEEKING.

Then I discovered I had ASKED, SOUGHT and KNOCKED, hoping to find the key to open the door.

Instead, the DOORKEEPER was that KEY, and . . .

"HE" was also the DOOR!

"Ask and you will be given what you ask for. Seek, and you will find. Knock and the door will be opened" (Matthew 7:7).

A Slice of Bread

Please, God
Keep me from becoming stale
   In the bread box of life,
Or stagnant in the oven of day-to-day living.

May I never become moldy
With self-pity,
Teach me to enjoy the blessings
   of others,
As I wait, wait such a long time
   For my slice of bread
On the table of time.

"Better it is to be of a humble spirit with the meek and poor, than to divide the spoil with the proud" (Proverb 16:19 AMP).

To Bend or Not to Bend

God,

I bow my arthritic knees before you. Help me lest the stiffness of these physical joints become a symbol of my spiritual self.

Keep me from the calcified spurs of indifference, that cause an unyielding stubbornness to change. A refusal to bend with the bends of life!

Let me be sensitive to others. I want to reach out to them with tenderness and compassion.

And please, God, when I get spiritually stiff, will you LIMBER ME UP.

※

"'For I know how rebellious and stubborn you are,' Moses told them" (Deuteronomy 31:27).

A Carousel of Dreams

The airplane of my dreams
Went round and round.
    As the carousel played an imaginary sound,
In my dizziness I fell to the ground.
    There in the dust I lay,
Exposed, dirty, afraid.

"I think I'll just stay here,
    Die in the sand."
"Oh no, how can I,
    Abandon my ship when it's about to land?"

So dusting the dust,
Determined to win
    I jumped back on,
Took hold of the controls
    That brought my dreams in.

*"Jehovah is my rock, my fortress and my Savior.
I will hide in God, who is my rock and my refuge.
He is my shield, and my salvation, my refuge and
high tower. Thank you, O my Saviour, for saving
me from all my enemies. I will call upon the Lord,
who is worthy to be praised "(2 Samuel 22: 2-4).*

Spiritual Vitamin

I'm working at it pretty hard today, Lord.
I seem to find no stopping place.
The dishes are not done—
    The beds are unmade.
I look like a freak—
    There have been a "jillion" interruptions.

To pause with you for a few brief moments
    Is somewhat like getting a vitamin shot.
The busy day moves along better
    After your strength absorbs itself
Into my spiritual life stream.

Sometimes, Lord, I find myself caught
    In this busy cycle of a spiritual merry-go-round
Just doing things.
    I've even fooled myself into believing
This to be spiritual maturity.
    My pride, my ego, loves to rotate itself
Around the wheels of my Christian service.
    It seems you've hidden your face from me!

TODAY—I WOULD SEE JESUS—P.S. I DID!

"Search me, O God, and know my heart; test my thoughts. Point out everything you find in me that makes you sad, and lead me along the path of everlasting life" (Psalms 139:13).

Falling Leaf

A falling leaf floated through the air,
Resting gently against my patio door.
It was the first to kiss autumn's early morning dew.
Come spring the leaf will live again.
A node, another piece of foliage will take its place.
Or will it?
The leaf did not really die!
It just gave of itself that the tree might live.
No one, nothing dies
Who dares make room for another's growth.
P.S.
"Teach me, O Lord, to give that others might live."

"And here is how to measure it—the greatest love is shown when a person lays down his life for his friends" (John 15:13).

Friendship's Garden

While walking through my Garden of Friends
   I stopped to rest for a bit.
To admire each floral beauty
   And the life it so aptly spent.
Turning my head in amazement
   Standing before my eyes
Was a daffodil gracefully lifting
   Its tiny face to the skies.
The poised serenity of its petals
   Calmed my heart that day.
The flower had been planted, by a friend
   Who knew I'd be coming that way.

A violet was blooming in perfect silence
   'Neath a tall and stately rose.
With no thought of being unnoticed,
   Serving in quiet repose.
The face of a sturdy sunflower
   Stooped, bending its leafy head.
A carnation whispered to it kindly
   About what the petunia had said.

Each flower was yielding its fragrance
   Giving its beauty free.
I stood . . . absorbing the perfumes
   My friends were imparting to me.

*"A true friend is always loyal and a brother is
born to help in time of need"* (Proverb 17:17).

(Taken from **Be The Woman You Want to Be** by Ruthe White, copyright © 1978,
Harvest House Publishers, 2861 McGaw, Irvine, Ca., 92714. Used by permission.)

Let Me Be Real

Well Lord,

I ask you to keep me from the sin of arrogance.

Help me that I shall never talk more than I am willing to listen.

Nor do I want to run further than I am willing to walk.

May I never want to teach others until I have first been willing to learn.

Put a guard on my mouth lest I profess more than I possess.

Let me be real!

I want to feel,

Feel with others: laugh with them, cry with them; and have them laugh and cry with me.

"Do things in such a way that everyone can see you are honest clear through " (Romans 12:17).

Kiss Me With Laughter

Please, God,
   Give my life the fragrance of a rose.
Kiss the petals of my personality with the dew of
   laughter.
   Fill me with the nectar of joy.
Let the honeybee draw from my supply.
   Make me so tender a child can delight in me.
   When I reach the time of old age,
May the posed serenity of Your grace be seen in me.
   Should there be any beauty on the vine of my life,
Let it live, be remembered with gladness,
In the hearts of those who nurtured me.

"Then was our mouth filled with laughter, and our tongue was singing (Psalm 126:2, AMP).

Return of the Raindrop

A raindrop whispered to me, crystalline, pure and serene
On my window sill, reflecting, a shining prism.
Soon it was nowhere, could not be found, on the window sill, or on the ground.
I searched for the raindrop, in the air, the atmosphere, everywhere.
The earth had opened its thirsty crust, swallowed, imbibed, gobbled it up.
It was lost in the soil, soon to become a rivulet, running stream.
Pouring into the ocean, giving, never receiving. In springtime I discovered anew, the raindrop, in the moisture of early dew.
I looked into a rose petal, a sparkle was there. The raindrop had returned, crystalline, pure, serene, it was everywhere.

"He sends the rain upon the earth to water the fields and gives prosperity to the poor and humble, and takes sufferers to safety" (Job 5:10, 11).

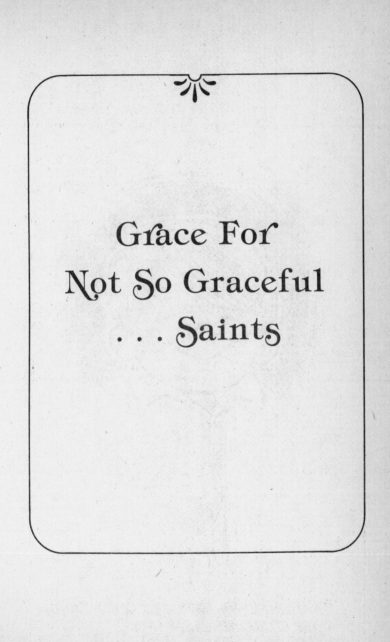

Grace For
Not So Graceful
. . . Saints

"And he said unto me, My GRACE is sufficient
for thee" (2 Corinthians 12:9, KJV).

Tired of Scrubbing Noses

I am tired of being a mother!

Tired of scrubbing noses that will be dirty again in seconds, and making beds that must be done over in a matter of hours.

Every closet I cleaned last week is needing it again today. The patio window, that was "sparkling" clean this morning, is already marred with freshly imprinted dog paws and children's fingerprints.

I was so proud of my "squeaky" clean floor until the baby threw his dinner off the high chair, and the cat spilled his milk.

"Why is life such an endless task?"

"You are tired, huh?" the Lord asked.

"Yes, and you had better believe it."

"All right, there are two hospitals in the city, which one would you choose?"

"That's not the point, I don't want to go to the hospital!"

"I see, you prefer one of the children go. In that case, which child would you assign to the pediatric ward?"

"Lord, you are so unreasonable! That is not what I mean."

"I see, the dog is your problem. That is easy enough to handle. I'll just put him to sleep" the Lord said.

"Can't you understand how much the dog means to my children. Heaven forbid you should do that."

"Well then, just what would you suggest?" the Lord inquired of me.

"I want one thing, one thing only!"

. . ."and what is that?"

"GRACE . . . grace to make beds, wash noses, clean windows . . . and love that French Poodle."

I Will

I have watched some people as they have learned to bury their past hurts, learning from the "LAW OF LIFE."

Others seem to try, but their wounds are so deep they do not heal quickly. I wonder why? Where does one go, and what does one person do that another does not?

Then I am reminded: It is the sick organism that refuses to heal. When a living, healthy body is given time and care, it will eventually heal itself!

If by chance the wound is so deep it cannot be healed by natural methods, it must be dealt with otherwise. Sometimes the opening needs to be stitched together, sutured by the "Great Physician."

Again, we must be aware that it is by our own effort and will that the bleeding wound is brought to the surgical table of God's healing hand. We must want healing from the problem, rather than learning to adjust to it.

If we bring our hurts to God, He has promised to cover the open wound with the "grafted skin" of his Living Word. When He does the work, it is complete! There are no scars . . .

. . . and no reminders to evoke the sympathy of others.

"Then they cry to the Lord in trouble and He delivers them out of distresses. He sends forth His word and heals them" (Psalm 107: 19, 20, AMP).

Friends Are People Too

My friends mean alot to me! God and good people have done much in helping me down the road of life.

For this I am grateful!

I am especially thankful for the friend who dropped me a note the other day. She was rushed and the message hurriedly scrawled. But it said so much!

It told me she cared, and that she was unafraid to expose her feelings.

Strange as it may seem, when I met her I never once thought a lasting relationship could develop. It was only a casual introduction. Besides, she appeared to me as being such a self-assured person, she would never need my friendship. I thought she needed no one, particularly me!

I have discovered everybody does need someone! It is just that I often pass them by without realizing it. Had this woman not made the first gesture of kindness, I would never have known the joy of her beautiful personality.

It is possible I have missed so much by waiting, waiting for someone else to prove they want my love or thinking they don't need it, when inside they are hurting for the lack of it. So what if they are from a background other than my own or come from another social circle?

It is important that I never take them for granted. Should I ever become so busy and absorbed in my own self importance that I cannot take time for friends: I then . . . will have lost the "JOY OF LIVING."

"Two can accomplish more than twice as much as one, for the results can be much better. If one fails, the other pulls him up; but if a man falls when he is alone, he's in trouble" (Ecclesiastes 4: 9-10).

Lesson From The Birds

A chirping bluebird swept through the air. With one cautious maneuver he retrived a grape that had been thrown onto the ground near our campsite.

Suddenly the air was alive!

His fluttering companions were quickly summoned to share in the loot. Some of his feathered friends watched while others "snitched." They were protecting each other; sharing, giving, as they spoke in animated chatter.

It was a touching scene. Such small creatures of the universe teaching me congeniality.

Hospitality!

Then, I watched a wealthy lady as she grasped her money while dying of malnutrition. She was too stingy to share in her own bounty. Not even with herself!

I stopped to pray:

"Lord, give me the reasoning of the birds."

"It is possible to give away and become richer! It is also possible to hold on too tightly and lose everything. Yes, the liberal man shall be rich! By watering others, he waters himself" (Proverbs 11:24, 25).

Not Another Sermon, Mom

What a "klutz" I am!

Why, when I am trying to help do I always get caught in the middle of things? I'm always wishing I had never given my opinion!

Could it be I have taken on a "Messiah" role? What makes me believe I have some great insight no other member of the family has? Perhaps, I have assumed, in the eyes of others, a "guru" position of exalted piety.

It may be that is the reason my children keep saying:

"Oh no, mom, not another sermon."

I keep wondering why they are so rude to me when I have such spiritual nuggets of truth to share with them. So, in my human weakness, I keep right on "rattling away," as if I have all the answers.

Finally, when out of my own brashness, my ego is deflated, I keep running to the Lord hoping He will understand me.

But why doesn't He say more to me than:

"Oh, stop your whimpering, and get that ironing done!"

"Let God train you, for he is doing what any loving father does for his children. Whoever heard of a son who has never been corrected?" (Hebrews 12:7).

God Never Puts Me On Hold!

"I am all choked up over missing your phone call! You just might reach me if you call this other number. Should you have a message for me, please wait until you hear the sound of the ducks and proceed with your recorded information."

"Quack! Quack!"

There were a few moments of silence between the last "quack" and when the mechanical device started humming. I knew that was my cue to talk back to the machine. But by the time the last duck gave his last quack, I had forgotten all prior information.

Rather than "flub" up the whole thing, I just stood there with phone in my hand saying nothing. Absolutely nothing! Thirty seconds later I heard the tape click off, as I was left "sputtering," wondering what had happened to the ducks.

By this time I had become terribly curious about getting through to the other number. I really wanted to speak with the man who left the recorded message. So, like an unlearned child, I dialed the long distance number.

"Hello, you have missed me again. You just might catch me, if you are persistent enough. Did you call my home . . . and did you hear the ducks? If you will leave me your information . . . and if the machine does not break down, I will return your call," the man said in his slow deliberate voice.

It had begun to seem like a game of telephone hide-and-seek! The person I was trying to find was evading me, then talking back to me from an impersonal black box. It was as if I was being placed on "hold" and my message was too unimportant to be returned; . . . or maybe the machine did break down. Anyway, there was never an answer from the other end of the line.

How very much like life this is. What one of us has

never called another, sending out a distress signal for help to receive nothing back except a cold mechanical reply. Or, maybe they didn't bother to answer us at all, too busy to become involved with where we hurt.

Sometimes they put us on "hold" too long! We are left standing to struggle through our own hurts until we become discouraged and "hang up."

Not so with God! He has never put me on "HOLD" while he took care of someone else. He always speaks "person-to-person," is always on time . . . and always returns my calls.

"He shall call upon me, and I will answer him" (Psalm 91:15, AMP).

Step Back Through Please!

"You, lady in the white suit, will you step back through the line, please," the airport security guard said.

I had walked up to the inspection center with smug assurance of having nothing on my person that would be the least bit questionable.

Suddenly, I was asked to go back through. Why?

They had detected a small piece of metal among my personal belongings! The photo scan was unable to identify it.

How embarrassing for me to stand there as they searched for the object. Soon they discovered it to be nothing more than a metal clasp that was holding my teaching charts together. What a small thing for such a "hassle."

But as I stood there, I was reminded of how often God looks into my heart, sometimes "zeroing in" on the least suspecting thing.

I know God will never touch my life for the sake of humiliating me. However, there are times when I feel like he is probing deeply into the hidden chasms of my inner soul. Often revealing things I do not want to see!

There are pieces of scrap metal resentment, criticism, and bitterness, that could well become lethal weapons to my better self. It is up to me to decide whether or not I wish to stand in line with the offenders of life . . . or to identify the arsenal.

"You spread out our sins before you—our secret sins—and see them all" (Psalms 90:8).

Puppets-On-A-String

Could it be we are little more than puppets-on-a-string? Is our culture creating within us a vacuum, a false sense of security through which we may placate our fears?

It seems to me we have become creatures of moods. Even the commercial world has recognized us as such. I am told the atmosphere of a business will sometimes determine its marketing strength; that by creating a pleasant environment, there is a kind of buying ease. We all know music is filtered through a medical office for the purpose of helping a patient relax. (And, I like that.)

But what about the future? Will we be conditioned to march to the cadence of an economic society? A materialistic trend of being told what to do, what to buy?

Already, the average three-year-old child is more conscious of name brands than most adults. That tells me something!

I must learn to do more than register the thoughts of others around me. I must be a "MOODSETTER" rather than just another person on the string of society!

"Don't copy the behavior and customs of this world, but be a new and different person with a fresh newness in all you do and think " (Romans 12:2).

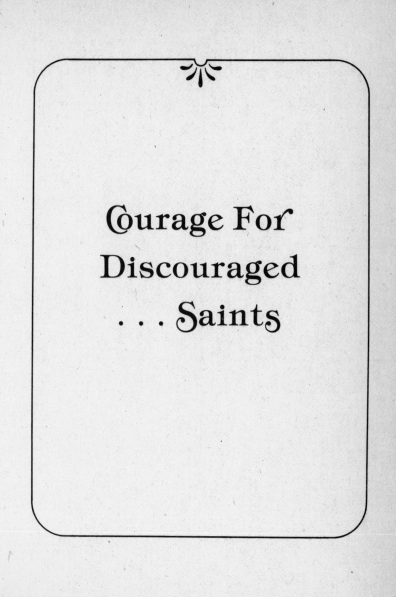

Courage For Discouraged ... Saints

I Am A Person

I am a person uniquely different, heriditarily, environmentally, and metabolically. Because I am unlike any other person in the world, there is a sense of originality about me. A freedom to move within the potential of my own God-given abilities.

I am free to be creative without feeling threatened by my peers. And I do not need to compare myself with any other.

With this relationship, between myself and the Heavenly Father, there comes a sense of personal worth. One that is neither egotistical nor self-debasing.

If I look only at my accomplishments, I become haughty and proud. If my failures are all I see, I become a martyr, stooped in self-pity, defeated before I begin.

Because I am what I am by the grace of God; and because His grace is unlimited, I too am unlimited. I am free to be an ongoing, growing, maturing personality.

My weaknesses and strengths must be measured together for a balanced approach to daily living: Otherwise, I will never be able to keep my head on straight in this . . .

```
C                    D                        D
  R                E                      L
    A          X                    R
      Z      I              U     O
        Y M                    P W
```

"If you, Lord, should keep account and treat (us according to our) sins, O Lord, who could stand (Psalm 130:3, AMP).

Nevertheless, Afterwards

The "afterwards" of life seem slow. Too slow! But they do come.

What are they?

They are the rainbows that follow the rain. The birth of a child after pain, and the healing that comes when the wounding is done.

Think of the calm after the storm or the victory on the heels of battle.

Put all of these together and you discover God's blessing of afterthought. Look at them alone, you see a beginning with no end, a storm with no rainbow, death with no hope of living.

Yes, the "afterwards of life" come slowly, too slowly for some of us. But again I remind you they do come!

"Being punished isn't enjoyable while it is happening—it hurts! But, afterwards we can see the result, a quiet growth in grace and character" (*Hebrews 12:11*).

Go Where?

What one of us has never felt the urge to walk out on the problems of life. We all have!

Even David, the Psalmist, was tempted to do so. He prayed: "Oh! that I had wings like a dove! for then would I fly away" (Psalm 55:6, KJV).

I have to ask you, "David, did you go?

"I hope you did not yield by running away from your problems. I trust you remained there and let time and God work things out for you.

"David, I have watched a lot of people run, running from themselves. They didn't resolve anything for they were their own worst enemy.

"No, you didn't go did you? I think you found the answer right in the middle of your troubles: Otherwise, you could never have written these words":

"Give your burdens to the Lord. He will carry them. He will not permit the godly to slip or fall" (Psalm 55:22).

Ride Higher

Early mariners tell stories of how they were very nearly wrecked on the great oceans of the world. The biblical apostle, Paul, speaks of a time when he and his companions were almost shipwrecked.

The scriptural account tells of how they threw their cargo overboard. It was done so the ship would not ride heavy!

There was only one way to survive the storm. That was to lighten the ship.

This is often true on the ocean of life. Our vessels get weighted down, become heavy with the apparent necessities of life. Yet, how unimportant they all seem when our lives are in danger.

Occasionally, the Lord has to remind us to throw off the petty little things that keep us down. He is most concerned that we do not sink. HE WANTS US TO RIDE HIGHER!

". . . let us strip off everything that slows us down or holds us back, and especially those sins that wrap themselves so tightly around our feet and trip us up" (Hebrews 12:1, TLB).

Little-By-Little

I sat aboard a great ocean liner and watched it cut a path across the Pacific Ocean. There were no visible markers for it to follow. The ship's direction was determined by the stars and the setting of the vessel's instruments.

What a sense of security that gave me!

I, too, had been launched on an unknown course in the ocean of life. There I was, left alone to find my way through the deep waters of my lonely experience. Everything around me looked threatening; the long, dark nights were foreboding, as wave after wave of disappointment lashed against me.

I was tempted to jump overboard. Abandon the ship! Progress was slow, not even visible to the eye. But it was coming!

Then, in the midst of the darkness, I looked up! There was the North Star, and I knew the spiritual compass of my life was headed in the right direction. With a hand of faith, I took a firm grip on the controls of the ship ploughing my way inch by inch, little by little, until the horizon appeared.

It was aflame with excitement and joy. Just beyond it's rainbow was land undiscovered, mountains to be climbed, new experiences that were to lift my spirits and steady my soul.

When my feet touched the shoreline of my unexplored dreams, I sighed from relief knowing:

The only thing that really matters, in the time of storm, is to keep faith's compass set in the direction of the "Morning Star."

He always remains constant!

"Where were you when I laid the foundations of the earth? Tell me, if you know so much. Do you know how its dimensions were determined, and who did the surveying? What supports its foundations, and who laid its cornerstone, as the morning stars sang together, and all the angels shouted for joy?" (Job 38:4-7).

God's Leftovers

There was a time when Jesus told his disciples to gather the scraps from off the table of grass. His followers picked up twelve baskets of leftovers.

The need became the challenge. By the simple relinquishment of the small supply into the hands of the Lord, it became a distribution of strength.

We don't always understand the calculated risk of giving everything to the Master. Yet, He in an orderly fashion has us "sit" and simply trust the matter to Him. The counting of the 5,000 who were to be fed was only an observation of the NEED. It had nothing to do with the possibility of the miracle.

The challenge became the mission. There was the demand for obedience. Christ always feeds but His mission is to fill the total need. He never does that until He has fully ascertained it.

So, I must believe:

1) That God not only feeds the multitudes around me. He also feeds me!

2) If He is interested in the multitudes, He is also interested in me. For, I am a part of that group.

3) When others are fed, I too, reap the benefits of His grace . . .

even if it's the LEFTOVERS!

"Do ye not yet understand, neither remember the five loaves of the five thousand and how many baskets ye took up" (Matthew 16:9, KJV).

Impulsive Love

"Catch it! Catch that ball!" the crowd roared. A batter had hit a foul ball. It was a "blooper" that sailed over the backstop and headed straight for the bleachers.

Three women were seated there: a mother holding her three-month old child, an expectant mother and a mother-in-law. Each one of them had been cheering her favorite player on.

Suddenly everyone was standing, waiting in dreaded fear! They stood helpless watching the ball speed through the air. It was coming toward the ladies with such velocity there was little time for action.

Its impact hit with a loud "thug" as the people waited in feared silence, wondering which of the women was injured. Or was it the baby?

No!

The mother had stretched herself across the body of the little one, taking the blow upon her own head. It dazed her momentarily, but her eyes were afire with joy, knowing she had saved the life of her child.

P.S.

Lord, help me to protect the person who is incapable of protecting himself. And, if by nature of my human weakness, I am unable to do so, may I never be guilty of hurling the ball that brings the injury.

"Woe to the man who does the tempting. If he were thrown into the sea with a huge rock tied to his neck, he would be far better off" (Luke 17: 1, 2).

Daily Bread

Thank you, Lord, for daily bread. The assurance of day-to-day sustenance. I am so glad life is planned that way; otherwise, I might squander your blessings.

Anyway, how could I know my needs or be able to project them into the future? There is no way! Only you are able to do that.

I cannot live on yesterday's blessings. They must be new each morning. So, I must come to you each day asking on the basis of my need for that day. And that day alone!

How very quickly those needs vary. Change!

Just twenty-four hours ago there was an air of serenity around our house, as my family ate the "BREAD" of your kindness in smug gluttony.

Not so today!

Life's normal interruptions have kocked at our domain. Sorrow, least suspected, has visited us. It came so unexpectedly, in such a short time.

Today, I ask only for today's bread. I want to eat the loaf you have especially prepared for me. To take it into my spiritual life stream, absorb every molecule of energy that is provided. To find "GRACE" necessary just for today!

I do not ask for tomorrow, tomorrow's needs will be different!

But . . . thanks, God, for the extra loaf you are cooking for me . . .

    . . . in the "OVEN OF YOUR LOVE."

"So don't be anxious about tomorrow. God will take care of your tomorrow too. Live one day at a time" (Matthew 6:34).

Hope For Hopeless

. . . Saints

Spiritual Amnesia

Is forgetfulness a sign of aging?

It must be!

Just yesterday I let the teakettle boil dry. The coffee pot was left on today.

How quickly I forget those things that are important, remembering to remember those that aren't. Is it really true that we recall only what we want to and forget what we don't want to remember?

I admit to sporadic lapses of memory and reoccuring attacks of ungratefulness. Or could it be spiritual amnesia? Whatever the reason, there are some things I have difficulty remembering.

I, like many others, often use the excuse of being so busy that the fault should be overlooked. Excused!

Sure I know it is true, life is cooking on all burners and there is something in every "POT" on the "STOVE OF LIFE" . . .

. . . But, excuse me please, I think I smell the pan of "THANKSGIVING" boiling dry.

". . . I will bless the Lord and not forget the glorious things he does for me" (Psalm 193:2).

A Cut Above Average

A friend once shared with me about the manner in which she had learned to trust other people. Having come from a wealthy background she had, by her own admission, considered herself a "cut above" the normal rung of society. Her childhood was spent in "aloofness," always probing to find the weak spots in others. She spoke of how she would "size" people up and then "zero in" on any weak area they might have.

Then . . . she was broken by a series of circumstances that leveled her. Years of humiliation, sorrow and finally social rejection led her to accept love from anyone around her, regardless of their status in life.

When I spoke with her she referred to those years of her life as a "place of privilege." The place where she learned the joy of appreciating people, accepting their kindness without scrutiny.

"Don't just pretend you love others; really love them. Hate what is wrong. Stand on the side of the good. Love each other with brotherly affection and take delight in honoring each other " (Romans 12: 9-10).

Rest in Peace

A stubborn old man plastered the outside walls of his hotel with signs. He was declaring war on the city fathers.

Today as I passed down his street, I observed a freshly painted message hanging there. It read:

"Rest in Peace."

I wondered who was resting. Did the old man give up in his long running battle for survival? Did he win, or did he just give up?

Perhaps I will never know. There is one thing I am very sure about—someone lost! It is even possible, as with most arguments, that no one is resting in peace.

Peace is not the child of bitterness and hate. When one person sets out to destroy another, regardless of the cause, it always results in someone being injured. In order for one to win, the other must lose!

P.S.

Lord, teach me to be decisive without becoming argumentative; to defend a cause without lashing out against the individual. Help me to love a principle more than I dislike the person involved . . . and to love that person even when he may differ with me.

"The beginning of strife is as when water first trickles (from a crack in a dam); therefore stop contention before it becomes worse and quarreling breaks out" (Proverb 17:14, AMP).

Man of the Celluloid Tape

A maturish looking woman wobbled along on her stilted wedge shoes, tripping carefully through the airport. Standing nearby was a cute little airline stewardess. (She kept blinking her artificial eyelashes.) Both were hoping to get a good look at the male movie star coming down the corridor.

People standing alongside were pushing with unbelievable rudeness, as they tried to move closer to the actor. A wave of the man's hand was his only response to the emotions of the scrambling crowd. Soon the attendants whisked him away to a private waiting room; insulating, protecting and isolating him from the frenzied crowd.

Sure there was a kind of thrill in coming face-to-face with such a well-known entertainer; yet, there was something about the incident that made me wonder. Did seeing one human being justify the shoving of the other? If we are all God's creation, how could we hurt one person to "deify" the other?

I question the value systems of our culture!

And . . . I pray that I might see the greatness of others without expecting the impossible from them. I want to know the thrill of finding a quality, even in the least suspecting person, and the joy of discovering it in those with whom I live daily, without minimizing it.

"If a man comes into your church dressed in expensive clothes and with valuable gold rings on his fingers, and at the same moment another man comes in who is poor and dressed in threadbare clothes, and you make a lot of fuss over the rich man and give him the best seat in the house and say to the poor man, 'You can stand over there if you like, or else sit on the floor'—well, judging a man by his wealth shows that you are guided by wrong motives" (James 2:2-4).

Poor Little Me

"Poor little me," the woman was saying. Her countenance spoke loud and clear; although no audible words were heard.

There was no sparkle in her eye, no spring to her step, just a "nagging" resonance about her voice. A kind of visible resentment could be seen through the sagging frown lines on her face.

She wore a cross around her neck as a symbol of inner freedom. When I saw it I expected to find a triumphant faith in the person wearing the silent testimony.

What a disappointment!

Instead of victory, there was defeat. Her inner spirit was exposed in the form of a self-crucifixion complex. The beauty of her witness was lost in her role of martyrdom.

How sad to find the cross a symbol of our living Lord, hanging around the neck of a dead (while living) saint.

"Dear brothers, is your life full of difficulties and temptations? Then, be happy for when the way is rough, your patience has a chance to grow. So let it grow, and don't try to squirm out of your problems" (James 1:2, 3).

I Am Human, Too!

I'm tired of being strong! Weary of being a leaning post. If people really knew how weak I was, they would never look to me for support.

But I am afraid to tell them!

Afraid to let them know I hurt too. I don't want anyone to know I struggle with some of the same problems everyone else does. It makes me look so good, so spiritual to pretend.

While I may not have all the answers to my own problems, I seem always to provide a few "pat" ones for other people. Surely this has not become some great ego-trip for me.

I wonder?

Have I made myself appear to others as a great pillar of strength, a spiritual authority standing with out-stretched arms, inviting people to look up to me?

I dare not tell them what I really am!

Perhaps, I should hide the fact behind a gilded layer of superficial piety.

If they only knew how fragile I was, how easily broken, they would never believe in me again.

Perhaps, perhaps not!

Maybe confession is what is needed. To allow myself to be exposed. Broken! Then there would be no reason for others to come to me or hold me in esteem.

Yes, that is it. Brokenness is what is needed—to lose the pieces of my own identity! Let self be lost so a new person can emerge.

. . . One that is honest, glued together with love, unafraid to be exposed and obviously human.

"Yes, Lord!"

"I am forgotten like a dead man, like a broken and discarded pot" (Psalm 31:12).

". . . they shall be shattered like a pot of clay that is broken into tiny pieces. And I will give you the Morning Star " (Rev. 2:27).

Life's Small Things

Today I count my blessings in the little things of life:
my home, family and friends.
There is the cry of a newborn baby.
The laughter of children playing in the street.
I feel the presence of God's warmth
In the sunlight, the kiss of morning dew.
There is an awareness of His presence in all of life,
Bringing hope and strength into my spiritual self.
He never promised to give me all my wants,
Although, sometimes he does.
God never quits giving to me.
Even in the routine things of day-to-day living.
All these are constant reminders of His love.
Sometimes I forget to say thanks
And am guilty of the sin of ingratitude,
Without enjoying the full benefits of each new day.
There is the temptation of wanting more,
While going in my own selfish way.

"Stay away from the love of money; be satisfied with what you have. For God has said, 'I will never, never fail you nor forsake you' " (Hebrews 13:5).

Who Chose Whom?

Thanks, God, for straightening me out. I had the whole concept of your plan upside-down and backward. I thought I had chosen you!

Not so!

You have chosen me from the foundation of the world. Since that is true, I cannot negotiate some big deal for your acceptance. There is simply no need or reason for begging Your favor.

It is a matter of simply accepting your offer.

Now I do just that!

I receive the benefits of Your grace without feelings of vague unworthiness.

Anyway . . . if you did the choosing, who am I to question your judgment?

"In Christ He chose us before the world was founded, to be dedicated, to be without blemish in his sight, to be full of love; and He destined us— such was His will and pleasure—to be accepted as His sons through Jesus Christ" (Ephesians 1: 4, 5).

Rest For Restless . . . Saints

Desert Solitude

The barren desert with its parched tumbleweeds, prickly cacti and spreading ocotillo is calling me.

It beckons me away from the busy rush of freeway traffic and the hustling demands of people, tugging upon me like the strings on a puppet longing to be set free.

It's the quietness of the desert, the muted whisper of the light summer breeze that calls to me out of this concrete jungle.

Lord, I wonder, is that the way you felt when you asked your disciples to go with you to the desert place and there come apart from the multitude?

P.S.
"Thanks, Lord, for understanding!"

"Even the wilderness and desert will rejoice in those days; the desert will blossom with flowers. Yes, there will be an abundance of flowers and singing and joy!" (Isaiah 35:1).

Rest, I Like That!

Thanks God,

. . . for giving me a resting time. You have provided us with many places for mental, spiritual and physical renewal. I thank you!

Rest, I like that! However, you never seem to provide a stopping place. Maybe it's for a reason.

I have never really wanted to stop! To quit trying, learning and growing. That would bring sudden death to me.

Resting times are fine so long as I don't become too comfortable in my situation and just want to sit down there: relax where I am and die on the vine of life. So, I am asking you God to keep working with me. When I get spiritually lazy, put me back to work. Keep "prodding" me into action, lest I have spiritual atrophy.

But please give me enough common sense to recognize your interruptions as being resting places!

"Now I can relax. For the Lord has done this wonderful miracle for me. He has saved me from death, my eyes from tears, my feet from stumbling. I shall live! Yes, in his presence—here on earth " (Psalm 116: 7-9).

Lord, I Give You Back
Your Shoes

My neighbor is ill from a heart attack. A friend of mine is struggling through a divorce. A daughter of mine is crushed from a disappointing blow in life itself.

How I wish I could help!

There are not enough hours in the day. Sometimes, I wish for just a few minutes more to give, another moment to share.

Come to think of it, God, you designed this universe with minutes on a twenty-four hour day schedule, didn't you? You must have had a reason. It could be I am out of "kilter" with your major plan.

Lord, are you trying to say something to me?

"Child, I created you with only two hands and feet.
I do not ask you to take on my responsibilities.
I never demand more than you can give.

"These problems are not yours. They are mine!
Your part is in bringing them to me. Mine is to honor the action of your faith."

"Thanks, God, what a relief to hear you say that. Here, I give you back your shoes of responsibility. They are much too big for me to wear."

P.S.
   Is that the reason I have been feeling so-o-o-o tired?

> *"Let him have all your worries and cares, for he is always thinking about you and watching everything that concerns you"* (I Peter 5:7).

Offshoots

One limb on the peach tree in our backyard shot out like a giant arm reaching into the heavens.

It seemed ahead of the others. Stretching, pulling, looking as if it were trying to attain some great height unknown to the other limbs. Its growth became more visible with each new day.

We watched it as its leafy head waved through the air. There was a kind of arrogance about it.

When fruit bearing season rolled around, we looked for fruit on the spindly branch.

There was none! Why?

Something had gone wrong. Waving in the wind had produced no fruit. Sure it had been seen! But, it was an offshoot that had never been pruned. Year after year it had done its thing as if independent of the tree itself.

All its energies were lost in its visibility. I was reminded that the fruit of the spirit is more than being seen or heard; it takes a lot of pruning, a gradual growth and the ability to produce more than leaves— leaves that soon drop away!

". . . and noticed a fig tree beside the road. He went over to see if there were any figs, but there were only leaves " (Matthew 21:19).

Monuments or Tombstones?

Yesterday I built a monument. When the statue was completed, my proud heart admired it.

Today I have built no monument! There has been little time for that. The day was spent in tearing away at the pieces of self-righteous piety that went into yesterday's action.

I thought I had built a monument that would stand, being long admired by those who knew me. Not so! Instead, it was little more than a tombstone. A cold slab cemented together with bits of insincerity. My good works being the foundation upon which it rested.

There was so much effort that went into the stone. Yet, I dare not leave it standing; for the monument speaks not of warmth and life. It is icy and angular!

Now that the edifice is broken and lies as dust under my feet, I stand with nothing to show for all my efforts. I feel naked, stripped of self, as I am exposed to the light of the Holy Spirit.

Tonight my selfish pride points to no great accomplishment of which I can boast.

But as I stand veiwing yesterday's mistake, I hear the Lord whispering:

". . . And the angel replied, 'Your prayers and charities have not gone unnoticed by God ' " (Acts 10:4).

P.S.
Thanks, Lord, I would rather have a memorial than a tombstone any day!

Things Are Looking Better

A friend of mine told of how she became extremely critical over a situation that existed in her church.

Nothing was going right in her opinion! The minister was no longer effective in the pulpit; choir members sang off-key; and the organist played the organ too loudly.

Out of her spirit of criticism, she became miserable. Her feelings of guilt soon isolated her from the body of spiritual believers.

During her time of struggle, she tells about finally resorting to prayer:

"Dear God," she said, "I don't like the way things are going around here!"

Then she enumerated all the negative aspects about the church, its minister, the choir and organist.

"God, please do something with these people around here," she prayed.

"Alright," God said, "I will begin with you first!"

"Oh no!," the woman cried, "Things are looking better already."

"Very well," God replied, "If you were marooned on an island all alone, dying, would you refuse help from any one of the persons you have mentioned?"

. . . and the lady said, "Forgive me Lord!"

"So don't criticize each other any more. Try instead to live in such a way that you will never make your brother stumble by letting him see you doing something that is wrong" (Romans 14:13).

Homesick For Love

Well, Lord, I come to you this morning as a friend. One whose fellowship I have missed. Could be I have not taken time to find you in the busy rush of my daily activities.

Today I want nothing from you. The pleasure of sitting at your feet is reward enough.

How I have missed those relaxed moments of listening to your voice, waiting in meditative thought for the whisper of your love.

It isn't that I have not wanted to do this more often! Somehow, the schedule of living has crowded in upon me. It pushes at me from within and without.

I know you are always there and my relationship with you is not changed.

I am just "HOMESICK FOR YOUR LOVE!"

"He brought me to the banqueting house, and his banner over me was love" (Song of Solomon 2:4, KJV).

Honey Bees

I chased a nest of bees and got stung; I received absolutely nothing for my work. Their honey was not even worth my efforts.

I watched a friend as she chased the bees of her life, going after them one by one. When she found the source of the problem it brought more trouble than happiness. A painful sting was left in the heart of her closest friend, causing much hurt, bringing embarrassment to all persons involved.

I saw another friend as she walked calmly through the disappointments of her life: loving one day at a time, solving each "pesky" problem as it came. She was borrowing no trouble, running after no "hearsay," keeping her own worries to herself.

That person was living! And, she was eating the sweetest honey from the nectar of her own serenity.

". . . and with honey out of the rock would I satisfy you" (Psalm 81:16, AMP).

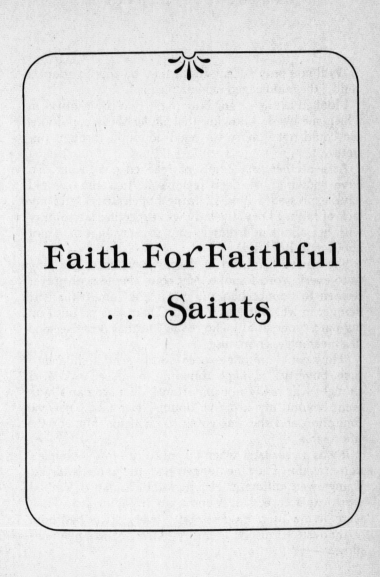

Faith For Faithful
. . . Saints

A Mother's Prayer

"Will you pray for me that I may be able to adopt a child," the middleaged woman pleaded.

I looked at the clean, but small, two-room hovel in which she lived; knowing that under those conditions she could not qualify for legal adoption through our state.

As a mother, my emotions reached out to her. To have shown those deep feelings at that time would have expressed a kind of futile hopelessness, and my lack of faith. I knew the lady was expecting me to pray with her about it. I didn't want to pray that day, not about that. But I did!

She bowed her head in deepest reverence, grasping onto every word I spoke. My cold, theological prayer seemed to bounce back at me in the same ritualistic manner in which it was uttered. There was no faith on my part. None at all! The request at that point seemed like meaningless nonsense.

"How could anyone expect God to send a child into such poverty?" I kept thinking to myself. What I thought was really not important! That woman's faith went beyond my negative doubts. Her God knew no limitation and she was going to challenge him for the impossible.

It was a year later when I went to call in the couple's home again. They no longer had the same address. Things were different! Her husband, a man of limited work experience, had found a good paying job. They were living in a modest, but lovely, two bedroom farmhouse, furnished them by her husband's new employer.

She had invited me there to share with them in the good news: "We are getting a baby in about three months," the lady said. Then she led me into a room already decorated with nursery furniture.

The baby boy arrived on schedule. They moved him into the house with all the fanfare of parents with a newly born child.

But that is not all the story, for in less than five years time a second boy was adopted into the family. What a joy it was to see them as they came to worship each week.

The mother would come to church wearing the same gingham dress and an ear-to-ear smile week after week. That didn't seem to matter because they had each other! Not once did I hear a complaint from her about stretched budgets, or the lack of what they did or did not have. She was too happy to miss the luxuries of material things.

Often during our worship services, I would "peek" at them from the corner of my eye just in time to catch the glimpse of a tear as it dropped from the mother's grateful cheek. Seated on the pew, on either side of her, were two healthy, squirming boys . . . adopted miracles of one woman's living faith.

"Children are a gift from God; they are his reward" (Psalm 127:3).

Timekeeper

God does not simply direct. He is the compass and the timekeeper.

Most of our feelings of being lost are because we have taken our eyes off the spiritual direction of our lives.

Somehow, we have begun to look at the earth instead of the stars. No timepiece is set by the position of the earth in itself; rather, by the position of the earth as it relates to the sun.

So it is when we gauge our progress and spiritual timing by the gravitational changes of people surrounding us. We may soon discover that they too are only rotating themselves around each other, setting timepieces of inner principle by what others are doing . . . never realizing . . .

. . . time is too important to overlook the . . .
"TIMEKEEPER."

"Praise him who made the heavenly lights, for his lovingkindness continues forever: the sun to rule the day, for his lovingkindness continues forever; and the moon and stars at night . . ." (Psalms 136: 7-9).

Others Hurt Too!

So what, God . . .
Every bone inside me is sympathizing with the other, begging to be released from the clutches of the flu bug.

True, every ache is a reminder of my human weakness and frailty. It is something more.

It reminds me that I must never become so absorbed in my own feelings and personal suffering that I have no sympathy for others. Pain must be kept in its right perspective. For I know when all the energies of my life are used in self-compassion, there is none left for sharing. When that happens, I will have lost the joy of living, the true value of life itself. Soon I will be covered with little more than self-pity.

Please, God, help me to bring happiness into the hearts of those around me. Give me the strength to share their burdens without constantly reminding them of mine. And if I am unable to lighten theirs, keep me from the temptation of adding more!

"But let every person carefully scrutinize and examine and test his own conduct and his own work . . . for every person will have to bear [be equal to understanding] his own load (of oppressive faults)" (Galatians 6: 4, 5 AMP).

The Computer and Me

"Am I anything more than a number on the computer of life?" Sometimes I wonder!

When I enter a store their hidden cameras photograph my every movement. As I check out at grocery counters, little black boxes talk back to me. Computers wring out data like a "bubble machine" spitting bubbles, telling my personal secrets!

I stand in dreaded fear as the sales persons "click" at the buttons on the contraption in front of them. I am wondering what the "thing" is telling the world about me.

Do I rate well? Perhaps fair, or maybe a poor risk!

All I can do is wait. Wait for someone hundreds of miles away to push another button that will tell the grocery clerk, who lives next door to me, what kind of person I am.

What an ominous feeling!

I keep hoping the "piece of metal" likes me.

What if it doesn't? I can't buy groceries! If I can't buy food, it doesn't really matter what the verdict is.

Come to think of it, I not only can't eat: I can't register to vote in order to change things; nor can I purchase much of anything vital to living without punching the secret numbers. That means I must be careful or the "little black box" will squeal; tell everything it knows about my bank account, where I live, and other no longer private information.

What a helpless feeling it is!

But wait, the computer is not the final authority of my life. There is another machine working. One that counts the very hairs on my head. (Someone once told me I have 90,000. Had I been born a blonde or redhead, they say the count would have been different.)

I speak of the "MASTER COMPUTER." The one that records my thought patterns: each word, deed, goes down on its pages of time. This is the recording device I am most concerned about!

Someday, I know, I will walk up to the counter of life and try to cash a check on the reserve of my past. When that happens, I hope some good data is fed back from the management of heaven, and that God OK's the transaction.

"For we must all stand before Christ to be judged and have our lives laid bare—before Him. Each of us will receive whatever he deserves for the good or bad things he has done in his earthly body " (2 Corinthians 5:10).

God Never Misses A Stitch

Athletes, real live masculine ones, thin skinny types, movie stars, executives and housewives have all taken up needlepoint.

"If they can do it, so can I," I kept saying outloud to myself.

Finally, I saved enough money from the grocery budget to buy thread, needle, a piece of the creative cloth and hoops for holding it securely in place. (I found a sales person likes to sell you the whole works.)

No sooner had I started on my venture toward creativity, when I became aware of the tedious task before me. There must have been a million little squares. But I set out to tackle them with patience and a limited amount of skill.

In-and-out, out-and-in, the needle went. It seemed like hours had passed before any amount of progress became visible. And when the rows of stitches started coming together, they were running in all directions: up instead of across, down rather than up. Nothing was making sense, no pattern or continuity was taking shape. The outlined rose petals were beginning to closely resemble a cactus garden.

"That's just the way it is supposed to look!" I convinced myself.

Yet, I was determined and very persistent about getting the piece finished. The longer I worked on the rosebud, the more it looked like the shattered remains of some unknown species.

After having finished the last stitch of needlepoint, it seemed appropriate that someone should admire it. So I ran into the den, and holding it up before my family gladly exclaimed:

"See you didn't think I could do it did you?"

"Do what?" one of the girls muttered.

My eyes snapped fire, "Your child will never get this when I am gone. Just you wait!"

"No mother, really, what is it supposed to be?"

" . . That's a rose, can't you tell? Anyone ought to be able to tell that's a rose," I snarled.

"Oh, I'm terribly sorry, but I honestly thought it was a cactus pattern," she volunteered to say.

I wanted to throw the thing at her until I looked at the handwork more closely myself. Upon examining the piece I discovered some of the stitches missing. It was easy to see, I had left out some basic ones which would have given the pattern its symmetry and balance.

Soon a few added threads began to make a difference. The rose pattern was standing out in bold relief. Strange how just a few threads could have made such a change!

And what a thrill it is to know GOD NEVER MISSES A STITCH in the pattern of our lives.

"My frame was not hidden from You, when I was being . . . curiously wrought (as if embroidered with various colors) in the depths of the earth" (Psalm 139:15, AMP).

She Stood Tall

　　My friend stood tall!
Her arms were like the branches on a tree.
They reached out, inviting others to gather 'neath
the shelter of her giving personality.
　　Others accepted her willingness to nurture them:
They swarmed her like nesting birds in search of
protection for their young.
　　She lived to give, to provide help, solitude
for those who needed her.

　　Winter broke in upon my friend one day!
Her once leafy branches drooped as they were caught
'neath the icy snow;
　　And the chilling wind of her own personal sorrow.
I looked for those she had once sheltered.
　　They were nowhere to be found.
Somewhere nearby they were feeding their young,
　　Living out their days in mirth and gladness,
Forgetting the one who had given so much to them.

Then came springtime!
　　My friend pulled herself toward the first rays
of the early sun.
　　Soon she was lifting her lofty branches, higher
and higher,
　　As if trying to reach the heavens.
By summer she was standing tall again.
　　My friend had learned to live,
To let time heal her wounds, and to gather strength
to "STAND TALL" for one more winter.

　　　*"His anger lasts a moment; his favor lasts for
life! Weeping may go on all night, but in the
morning there is joy "* (Psalm 30:5).

Seasons For Seasonal . . . Saints

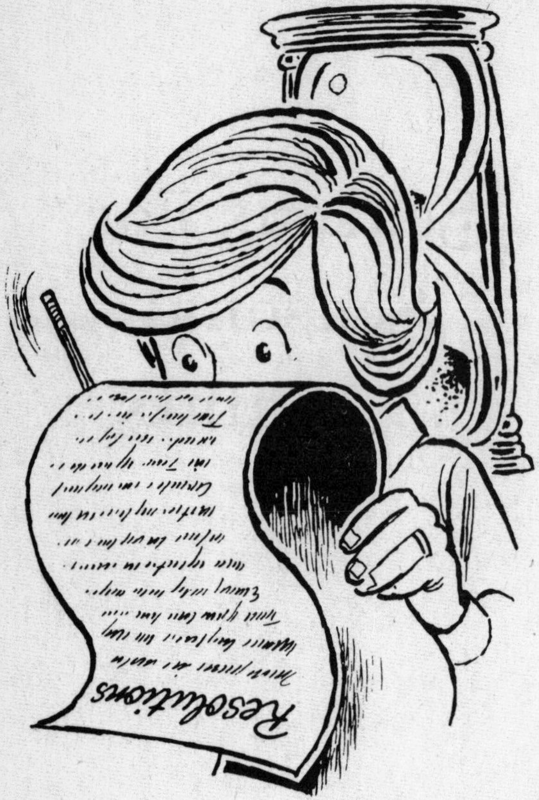
Resolutions

New Years

What, Lord, shall I offer you as a New Year's resolution? Do I dare make one more promise that may soon be broken, sometimes through neglect? Or, by plain human error?

Somehow, I cannot believe the answer to life is always found in simply turning over another new leaf (While that is not a bad idea). I must confess: There are discoveries on last year's leafy resolutions that are still speaking to me.

Should I overlook the principles of yesterday's leaf to pick up the new and exciting things for today? Do I dare, while in the blast of a New Year's celebration or in one emotional moment, vow to forever make a change. A change that may last no longer than the blowing of the whistles that herald in another day, another year.

True, Lord, I know there are certain weak areas of my life. And . . . this is a wonderful time for new beginnings. But please, God, help me that I will not become discouraged by remembering these are the very same problems that "baffled" me last year.

While I may not have scaled all of yesterday's mountains, here I am on the eve of a new year still climbing, learning and remembering that the Creator of time promises me strength for each new day.

So . . . I promise to quit turning over new leaves as if looking for some magic formula. But, to start examining each new day. Perhaps, beneath its leaf there I will discover your fingerprint . . . the fingerprint of God.

"God who called you to become his child, will do all this for you, just as he promised" (1 Thessalonians 5:24).

" 'This is it!' Adam exclaimed, 'She is part of my own bone and flesh! Her name is "Woman" because she was taken out of a man.' This explains why a man leaves father and mother and is joined to his wife in such a way that the two become one in person" (Genesis 2:23, TLB).

Valentine Love

I speak not of life
Without first thinking of love.
  For life is loving,
  Loving someone,
Someone with whom I share
  My moments of triumph
  And defeat.
One whose hand gently touches mine,
  In silence,
  Yet saying so much!

I love to see the twinkle
  In the eye of that someone,
Who responds instinctively to me,
  Because he loves the me
  Inside of me.
That person he knows so well,
  Whose secrets
  He will not tell.

I long to hear the sound of that someone's footsteps
  Racing across my threshold,
  Running against time,
  Savoring each moment of our aging,
  Growing,
  Mellowing love.

I want that someone to be near me,
  As he has always been
  Since then,
  When?
Our young hearts were joined,
  Entwined,
  Combined,
  United in time,
So many years ago.
  My husband . . . my VALENTINE.

Springtime

It's springtime!

The smell of orange blossoms filter through the air, as the wind plays hide-and-seek around my lilac bush. It is like the sound of a great musician fingering the strings of his violin.

There is a yellow rosebud half-closed, half-open outside my window. The flower looks as if it is afraid, embarrassed to show its face, too shy to lift its tiny petals toward the sun.

I feel like that rosebud!

Half afraid, daringly, after the long winter months of life's pruning, I struggle to look up to God. All these days, I have waited, absorbing the soils nutrients, longing for the first burst of springtime.

Finally it has come!

Now I must break loose, clothe myself with the freshness of a new beginning. It is time to open the closed petals of my life, to turn myself toward the "SON" and forget the bitter struggle of yesterday's winter. This brings with it a new challenge, a challenge for today!

There is a question: I wonder about the fragrance of my life. Will springtime produce an aroma of newness, or will there be an odor of dry musty leaves . . . left there, buried somewhere, beneath an unforgiving spirit?

"Arise, shine; for thy light is come, and the glory of the Lord is risen upon thee" (Isaiah 60: 1, KJV).

Easter

Jesus had been a guest in the home at Bethany many times before. On that day things seemed to be different! There was a forebooding cloud of darkness that hovered over them. A sense of impending danger filled the air. It was a silent almost ominous feeling.

Many people were in the home that night. The disciples of Jesus were among the crowd. But only one person, a woman, felt the soul needs of "MY FRIEND."

It was Mary whose intuitive heart motivated her to action. While the others sat relaxing in conversation, she slipped quietly away, then quickly returned. In her hand she carried an alabaster box of perfume. There was no announcement of her intentions. She sounded no trumpets, sought advice from no one, but went straight to the place where Jesus was sitting. The container was then broken, its valuable contents poured upon the head of the Master.

It was the most precious gift the woman owned! We are told the perfume represented one full year's wage. The oils were taken from the Himalayas. To the oil base was added the attar of 400,000 full grown roses. The translucent vase was broken. It lay at the feet of Jesus, a symbol of uninhibited love to the Master.

When the stingy crowd observed her unselfish act, they scolded her openly. It was "HE" who defended Mary by saying: "Let her alone, for against the day of my burying hath she kept this" (KJV).

Now, almost 2,000 years later, I can still smell the fragrance of her unselfish act. It rises as a perpetual incense in the hearts of all those who seek to worship the risen Christ.

"Then Mary took a jar of costly perfume made from essence of nard, and annointed Jesus' feet with it and wiped them with her hair. And the house was filled with fragrance" (John 12:3).

When God Made Mothers

. . . He made them as something special!

Their hands are delicately formed; they can create an exquisite piece of art while binding the imaginary wound of a child's broken heart. A mother's soothing touch to a feverish brow is like a "magic cure" to the inner soul.

True, her heart was placed inside a physical frame; yet, it knows no limitations as such. A mother's blood is pumped by love itself into every artery of life. The influence of her power is far reaching. Like capillaries of the human body, the pulse of her heartbeat is felt in the factory, business, church and in the Oval Office of the President.

Kings have been transfused by the plasma of her dreams. Nations are still being conquered through the inspiration of her ideals. Weak leaders are often supported by her feminine mystique. Her offspring have walked on the moon, tilled the soil, explored planets and plumbed the ocean depths.

She is a paradox! Unpredictable. Not easily understood by the male species. They have studied her, used her body, written pages of scientific data about her. Yet, no one has discovered the mystery of the woman herself.

Nor will they ever!

I ask you: "Can you foretell a woman's future, or measure the potential of her strength?"

God and God alone is able to contemplate her worth. For it was she He chose to bear His Son, tutor Him in childhood and to minister to Him at the cross.

She was the very last of all God's creative acts. When He had finished with His original "MASTERPIECE" called woman, it was as if God said:

"Now that I have made mothers, I can rest" . . .

He entered into the Sabbath to think.

"A woman that feareth the Lord shall be praised. Give her of the fruit of her hands, and let her own works praise her in the gates" (Proverb 31:, KJV).

Daddy Was a Millionaire

My father was wealthy. Extremely so!

People would often look at him surprised that a man with only a third grade education could amass such a vast fortune during his lifetime. They even questioned his investments; and at times, I felt daddy wondered about them himself.

Yet, he never talked much to anyone about what he did or did not have. His assets always remained a deep secret into which no one dared to probe. However, those who knew our family never doubted the fact that dad ruled an empire.

What people around us did not know was that my father owned and operated his own money mint! The federal govenment never suspected him. Not once did they investigate his corporation. We children looked, week after week, month upon end, hoping to find the place he might have stockpiled his reserves We kept finding where he had made small deposits. They were usually hidden everywhere, sometimes in the least suspecting places. He was always making some kind of new investments, often with the most unlikely persons. He always said:

"I am depositing in stocks with slow—but sure—dividends."

No, my father's wealth was not a monetary one and he didn't really own a mint. His riches were not even in the land he farmed. It was in the abundance of his own inner principle.

Integrity was the "gold mine" of his reserve strength. His word was better than his money, and his signature was a seal of honor.

Dad stacked and trusted his life's savings in a "Depository" opened with the key of human love. For he was a man who loved, loved deeply. It was shown openly as the "coins of kindness" flowed from him freely. Each kind deed and warm act was imprinted with the sweat of his own strong hands, as he held firmly to the trust of his friends who gathered around him. It was those same muscles and gnarled hands that "eked" out the family's living.

His life was short. He went to the grave prematurely! We always thought the reason he died so soon was because he invested more of his energies in others than he kept for himself. But now he lies buried in a poor man's grave.

Yet, he amassed a fortune!

A wealth of memories live on in the hearts of those who knew him. Years have come and gone now, but the accrued interest rate of his rich life continues to climb, as we remember the man who invested in the stock market of time and other people's lives.

No, daddy was not a wealthy man in terms of money, but . . .

. . . "MY DADDY WAS A MILLIONAIRE!"

"Better is a little that the (uncompromisingly) righteous man has, than the abundance (of possessions) of many who are wrong and wicked" (Psalm 37:16, AMP).

Thanksgiving

Ten sick men sat on the roadside begging. They had been sitting there for hours. Their tin cup was held up in hopeful anticipation as each tourist came near them.

Suddenly, the noise of a crowd filled the air. People were clamoring, pushing back and forth through the throng. Each one wanted to get closer; to hear what the man near them was saying.

It is understandable! This was not an ordinary man they were following. Jesus was walking with them! His words were worthy of their attention.

Afar off, the cries of the sick men echoed through the air. They cried out, "Jesus, Master, have mercy on us."

And when He saw them, he said unto them, "Go show yourselves unto the priest," The men took off running and as they went, they were healed.

. . . Only one of them returned to say "Thanks."

"... And as they entered a village there, ten lepers stood at a distance, crying out 'Jesus, sir, have mercy on us!'" (Luke 17:11).

When God Made the World

When God made the world
He made it round.
   Wrapped it in a protective tissue of soft clouds,
Sprinkled it with stardust,
   And tied it with a ribbon of delicate blue.

   When God wanted man
To understand His love,
   He searched for the brightest star
Of His creative workmanship.
   One whose radiant beams would penetrate the world,
Even the darkest part!

   When God found that "Bright Star"
He sent it into the world.
   The beauty of its glow touched all mankind
Encircling them with God's love.

   When God made the world
He left no corners in which prejudice or hate could hide.
   He took everyone into the circle of his love.
Everyone includes me.
   Even me!
When I worship the God who made the world,
   I rejoice in knowing God never draws circles to keep
   people out.
People do that!

"For God loved the world so much that he gave his only Son so that any one who believes in him shall not perish but have everlasting life " (John 3:16).

T'was the Week After Christmas

Hans, the dog, lies cowered beneath the tinsel of our bedraggled looking Christmas tree. He has overindulged himself on the fatty remains of leftover Christmas scraps. (Come to think of it, the whole house looks like the way the dog seems to feel.)

Our grandbaby has eaten the velvet "fuzz" from off the heads of the reindeer, that once pranced themselves across the lower limbs of the old plastic evergreen. (The one that stood so erect the first evening it was decorated.) It has bent its head lower and lower with each passing day, as if laughing back at me from the heated rush of the season. The crisp red bows, that adorned its branches three short weeks ago, are hanging like dishclothes, draping unevenly against its boughs.

However, those are not the things that "bugged" me most during the holiday season!

It was, and still is, those ominous blinking lights that keep grinding at my conscience. Why? Is it because each time I tried to shake, feel or secretly peek at a Christmas package under the tree, the red light on the limb in front kept shooting forth some "gamma" like ray? Perhaps, that is the reason I have been held so guiltily spellbound.

"Just you wait! Now that the gifts are all opened, it is my turn for revenge." (I have just pushed the sleeping dog from beneath the debris.) "That on-again-off-again light is going to catch it," I muttered outloud to myself.

With one turn of the wrist, I reached down and unsocketed the red light bulb.

"But why did the thing 'hiss' back at me?"

Could it be the last flicker of its light was a reminder of something to me? Something about life, priorities and the needs of others? Needs that cannot be boxed or wrapped in tinsel.

I keep feeling human needs as they are being signalled back to me, begging to be heard, loved and served. And

. . . there is a kind of "gamma" like ray that is holding me guiltily spellbound.

P.S.

Please, Lord, forgive me and make me sensitive to the needs of those about me.

"But if someone who is supposed to be a Christian has money enough to live well, and sees a brother in need, and won't help him—how can God's love be within him?" (1 John 3:17).

Papa's Stocking

The garage has just become the recipient of neatly packed boxes. Among the things boxed is "Papa's oversize Christmas stocking. (The one I hurriedly designed to match his personality.) Sticking out of a black, laced-up boot is a "knobby" knee. On it was sewn a small green golfing tee, with a not quite hole-in-one, struggling to hit the pin.

That along with all the other things: the musical angels, three unfinished hand-painted wisemen (. . . that I started six Christmases ago), garland and poinsetta china pieces, are all among that storage.

Actually, they may never be lifted to their reserved spot in the loft area of the garage. Usually they remain like a lady-in-waiting until we discover there is really no need of putting them away. We are too close to another season by that time.

The house looks almost naked without all of them. I miss the singing chimes and mistletoe especially. But there is a good feeling in knowing that before me is the simplicity of a room uncluttered. One whose decor I can live with for another year.

So, as I enjoy the thrill of placing the antique clock back on the old desk, where it sits the other eleven months out of the year, I cannot help but say:

"Thanks, Lord, for those things that are stable. And when the tinsel of life has lost its temporary value, it is so good to know you are constant, abiding . . . and still there."

"But whatever is good and perfect comes to us from God, the Creator of all light, and he shines forever without change or shadow" (James 1:17).